Tiny Talks

Volume 10
My Savior, Jesus Christ

**A year's worth of simple messages
that can be given during church
or family home evening**

Other children's books by Lee Ann Setzer

I Am Ready for Baptism
A fun activity book for children preparing for baptism.

Sariah McDuff: Primary Program Diva
The annual Primary program in sacrament meeting seems like the perfect place for Sariah to try out her new superstar rock singer act!

Sariah McDuff: Christmas Detective
What do you get for the girl who doesn't want anything that most kids want? Sariah, her offbeat family, and her funny Primary class find the true spirit of Christmas.

Sariah McDuff: Valentine's Day Scrooge
What is the true meaning of Valentine's Day if you're seven years old and you hate boys?

Sariah McDuff Will Walk with You
The Primary president wants Sariah to make friends with a girl who's very different.

Volume 10
My Savior, Jesus Christ

A year's worth of simple messages that can be given during church or family home evening

by Lee Ann Setzer

CFI
Springville, Utah

ISBN: 978-1-59955-375-7

Published by CFI,
an imprint of Cedar Fort, Inc.
2373 W. 700 S, Springville, Utah, 84663
www.cedarfort.com

Cover design © 2009 by Lyle Mortimer

Printed in the United States of America
10 9 8 7 6 5 4 3 2 1

Printed on acid-free paper

Table of Contents

Introduction

Welcome to Tiny Talks Volume 10!

This year's Primary theme is "I know my Savior lives." As we study the life, miracles, and example of Jesus all year, we can come closer to Him and feel His spirit.

This book of talks can be helpful "in case of emergency"—when someone forgot until Sunday morning that he or she was supposed to give a talk at church! But it can also be a useful resource for family home evening and family and personal scripture study. Each Tiny Talk includes a story, a thought question, a scripture, and a visual aid suggestion. This year, families have two Church-produced options for visual aid sources: the Gospel Art Picture Kit (GAK) and the new Gospel Art Book (GAB). I've listed visual aid ideas from both of these, when they were available.

I especially hope that children will enjoy reading this little book and looking at these wonderful pictures, just for fun.

—Lee Ann Setzer

Chapter 1

I Know Heavenly Father Loves Me

1. I Am a Child of My Heavenly Father

Scripture

Moses 1:16 — Get thee hence, Satan; deceive me not; for God said unto me: Thou art after the similitude of mine Only Begotten.

When Moses became a prophet, Heavenly Father showed him a vision. Moses saw God. He also saw the history of the whole world, from its beginning to its end. He saw you, me, and everyone who would ever live on it. He understood the whole plan of salvation.

When the vision ended, Satan appeared and told Moses to worship him. He called Moses a "son of man." But Moses answered, "Who art thou? . . . I am a son of God" (Moses 1:13). Moses could judge between God and Satan. He knew how he felt in God's presence. He knew he was Heavenly Father's child, and he told Satan to go away (see Moses 1).

Like Moses, we are children of our Heavenly Father. When we follow His plan for us, we can judge between right and wrong and make choices that will help us be happy.

Visual Aid:

GAB 3: The Earth/GAK 600: The World

Thought Question: How does knowing you are a child of God help you judge between right and wrong?

2. This Is My Beloved Son

When Jesus Christ died in Jerusalem, there was a terrible storm and many disasters in America. Mountains rose up, cities burned down, and terrible earthquakes shook the land. Then there were three days of thick darkness. The prophets had told the people that these disasters would come when Jesus died. When the darkness cleared, they gathered at the temple, talking about Jesus. Then everyone heard a voice in their hearts: "Behold my Beloved Son, in whom I am well pleased" (3 Nephi 11:7) It was the voice of Heavenly Father introducing Jesus Christ.

Jesus Christ is the Son of God. In the scriptures, Heavenly Father always introduces Him this way. Jesus made the earth for us. He came here to show us how to live. And He died for us, so we can return to Heavenly Father. We can trust and follow Jesus Christ, the Son of God.

Thought Question: Share your feelings about Jesus Christ, the Son of God.

Scripture

3 Nephi 11:7 — Behold my Beloved Son, in whom I am well pleased, in whom I have glorified my name—hear ye him.

Visual Aid:

GAK 82: Jesus Teaching in the Western Hemisphere/ GAK 315: Christ Appears to the Nephites

3. Ye Are of More Value than Many Sparrows

Scripture

Luke 12:7 — But even the very hairs of your head are all numbered. Fear not therefore: ye are of more value than many sparrows.

There are over six billion people on earth right now. Every one of us is a child of Heavenly Father. It's hard for us to imagine how He can know each one of us and hear each person's prayers. But Jesus taught, "Are not two sparrows sold for a farthing? and one of them shall not fall on the ground without your Father. . . . Ye are of more value than many sparrows" (Matthew 10:29, 31).

Heavenly Father knows everything about us—even the number of hairs on our heads! He also knows how we feel and what we need. Even when we feel alone, Heavenly Father is always watching and ready to help.

Thought Question: How do you know that Heavenly Father loves you?

Visual Aid:

None

4. He Took Their Little Children, One by One

When Jesus visited the people in America after His resurrection, He taught them at the temple all day. At the end of the day, He told them to go home and think about the things they'd learned. But no one wanted Jesus to go. So Jesus stayed. He healed all their sick and injured people. Then He called for the little children. He told the people to kneel, and He prayed for them all.

Jesus took each child, one by one. He blessed them and prayed for them. Jesus wept for joy because of the people's faith and love. Then angels came from heaven to bless the children.

Though we can't see Jesus, we can still feel His love for us—one by one. He still rejoices in our faith and love.

Thought Question: How have you felt love from Heavenly Father and Jesus?

Scripture
3 Nephi 17:21 — And when he had said these words, he wept, and the multitude bare record of it, and he took their little children, one by one, and blessed them, and prayed unto the Father for them.

Visual Aid:
GAB 84/ GAK 322: Jesus Blesses the Nephite Children

5

Chapter 2

My Savior and Redeemer, Jesus Christ

1. Whom Say Ye that I Am?

Scripture

Luke 9:20 — He said unto them, But whom say ye that I am? Peter answering said, The Christ of God.

During the week before Easter, three-year-old Wendy's mom was teaching the family about the last week of Jesus' life. "Mom," Wendy asked, "why did Jesus die for us?"

"Because He was the Son of God, and only He could save us," Mom answered.

"But, Mom," Wendy said. "Why did Jesus die for us?"

"Because," Mom said, "we all commit sin, and we all need His help."

"But, Mom," Wendy said. "Why did Jesus do that for us?"

Mom paused. All her answers were correct, so why did Wendy keep asking the same question? She gathered her little girl into her arms. "He died for us because He loved us, sweetheart."

Wendy smiled. Mom had finally found the answer that made her heart happy.[1]

Thought Question: Why did Jesus die for us?

Visual Aid:

GAB 1: Jesus Christ/ GAK 240: Jesus the Christ

2. The Lost Sheep

In the third article of faith, we learn that "through the Atonement of Christ, all mankind may be saved." Jesus told a story about what this means. Imagine that a shepherd had one hundred sheep, but one got lost. Jesus said that the shepherd would leave the ninety-nine other sheep in a safe place and go looking for the one lost sheep until he found it. He would lay it on his shoulders and come home to tell everyone how happy he was that he had found his lost sheep (see Matthew 18:12–13, Luke 15:4–7).

Jesus suffered and died for everyone's sins. He wants everyone to learn of Him, obey Him, and be saved. Almost everyone is not enough for the Savior. He loves each one of Heavenly Father's children, and He wants everyone to come to Him and be saved.

Thought Question: How can I help find Heavenly Father's lost sheep?

Scripture

Matthew 18:12 — How think ye? if a man have an hundred sheep, and one of them be gone astray, doth he not leave the ninety and nine, and goeth into the mountains, and seeketh that which is gone astray?

Visual Aid:

GAB 64: Jesus Carrying a Lost Lamb

3. Living Water

Scripture

John 4:14 — But whosoever drinketh of the water that I shall give him shall never thirst; but the water that I shall give him shall be in him a well of water springing up into everlasting life.

Jesus stopped at a well and asked a woman for a drink of water. He told her that if she had known who He was, she would have asked Him for living water. The woman did not understand. Jesus had no water bucket. Where would He get this living water? Jesus said that whoever drank from the well would get thirsty again, but "the water that I shall give him shall be in him a well of water springing up into everlasting life" (see John 4:3–30).

The ordinary water in this story is like our efforts to save ourselves. No matter how hard we try, we can't make ourselves perfect or forgive our own sins. The living water from Jesus is His Atonement. Because He is perfect, He can save us, and because He loves us, He suffered for us, and He gave us eternal life.

Thought Question: Share your feelings about the Savior Jesus Christ.

Visual Aid:

GAB 36: Jesus and the Samaritan Woman/ GAK 217: Woman at the Well

4. The Road to Emmaus

After Jesus died, His followers didn't understand that He would be resurrected. They felt lonely and very sad. They heard that Jesus' tomb was empty, but they didn't believe that Jesus was resurrected.

Soon afterward, two of Jesus's followers were walking down the road to the village of Emmaus. A stranger joined them and asked why they looked so sad. They explained how Jesus had died. The stranger told them that Jesus had to die first in order to be resurrected. He told them to believe in Jesus. They invited the stranger to come and tell them more. But halfway through dinner, the stranger vanished, and they realized they had been talking with Jesus.

When they hurried to Jerusalem to tell the apostles, Jesus appeared to them and commanded them to tell the whole world that He was resurrected. All their sadness turned to joy (see Luke 24).

Thought Question: Imagine you lived before anyone had heard about Jesus' Resurrection. How would you feel if you saw Him alive again?

Scripture
Luke 24:39 — Behold my hands and my feet, that it is I myself: handle me, and see; for a spirit hath not flesh and bones, as ye see me have.

Visual Aid:
GAB 60/ GAK 234: Jesus Shows His Wounds

Chapter 3

Follow the Prophet

1. God Calls Enoch to be a Prophet

Scripture

Amos 3:7 — Surely the Lord God will do nothing, but He revealeth his secret unto his servants the prophets.

Enoch was an ancient prophet. When God called him, Enoch was afraid. He said, "All the people hate me; for I am slow of speech" (Moses 6:31). He didn't think he could be a good prophet, but the Lord told him to go out and speak to the people. He promised to help Enoch deliver His message. He promised to protect Enoch and give him great power.

Enoch trusted the Lord. He preached to the people. Even though they made fun of him and tried to kill him, He still gave them God's message. His words were so powerful that he even moved a mountain! After many years, Enoch and his followers became so righteous that God took them into heaven (see Moses 6–7). Enoch's words were weak by themselves, but with God's help, Enoch could do everything the Lord asked him to do.

Thought Question: What can you do to follow the prophet?

Visual Aid:

GAB 6: City of Zion Is Taken Up/ GAK 120: Enoch and His People Are Taken Up to God

2. The Prophet Nephi Testifies of Jesus Christ

When Nephi in the Book of Mormon heard his father prophecy about Jesus Christ, Nephi wanted to know if his father's words were true. When he asked God, he received a vision like his father's. Nephi saw Jesus' birth in Jerusalem. He saw Jesus' mother, Mary. He saw the miracles and the teachings of Jesus. Then he saw the people crucify Jesus. He saw Jesus appear to the people in America.

Nephi understood Heavenly Father's plan of salvation and the Savior's love for all His people because he saw it. He spent the rest of his life teaching his family about the things that he had seen and felt. He testified of the Savior (see 1 Nephi 11–12).

Like Nephi, all prophets—in the scriptures and our prophet today—testify of Jesus Christ.

Thought question: Have you heard or read about the prophet's testimony of Jesus Christ?

Scripture

1 Nephi 11:20–21 — And I looked and beheld the virgin again, bearing a child in her arms. And the angel said unto me: Behold the Lamb of God, yea, even the Son of the Eternal Father!

Visual Aid:

GAK 301: Lehi's Family Leaving Jerusalem

3. Look and Live

Scripture

Alma 33:19 — Behold, he was spoken of by Moses; yea, and behold a type was raised up in the wilderness, that whosoever would look upon it might live. And many did look and live.

When Moses was leading the people of Israel through the wilderness, they were attacked by fiery flying snakes. Anyone that the snakes bit, died. The people cried to Moses for help, and Moses asked the Lord what to do.

The Lord told Moses to make a flying snake out of brass and mount it on a long pole. The people only needed to look up at the brass snake, and they would live.

Many of the people obeyed Moses. They looked up at the brass snake, and the real snakes didn't bite them. But some people were too proud or angry to look up. Those people were bitten by the snakes and died (see Numbers 21:4–9).

Just like the people in Moses' time, we have a prophet who listens to the Lord. If we follow what he says, we will be safe from Satan's temptations.

Thought question: Why wouldn't some people listen to Moses? Why won't some people listen to the prophet today?

Visual Aid:

GAB 16/ GAK 123: Moses and the Brass Serpent

4. God Speaks through Abinadi

Abinadi was a Book of Mormon prophet. God sent him to preach to wicked king Noah and his priests. King Noah was angry when Abinadi came to him. The priests wanted to have Abinadi killed. But Abinadi stood before the king and his priests in chains. He told them that God had sent him with a message, and he would deliver it before they killed him.

Abinadi taught them the Ten Commandments. He taught them about Jesus Christ and the plan of salvation. He taught them about their own sins and wickedness. When Abinadi finished his message, the king and his priests were so angry that they had Abinadi burned. Fortunately, a priest named Alma repented. He escaped and wrote down Abinadi's words. He preached about Jesus Christ and helped save many people (see Mosiah 11–13).

God spoke through Abinadi, and He still speaks through our prophets today.

Thought question: What blessings have you received because God speaks through His prophets?

Scripture
Mosiah 13:2–3 — And they stood forth and attempted to lay their hands on [Abinadi]; but he withstood them, and said unto them: Touch me not . . . for I have not delivered the message which the Lord sent me to deliver.

Visual Aid:
GAB 75/ GAK 308: Abinadi Before King Noah

Chapter 4

Joseph Smith and the Restoration

1. The First Vision

Scripture

James 1:5 — If any of you lack wisdom, let him ask of God, that giveth to all men liberally, and upbraideth not; and it shall be given him.

When Joseph Smith was a boy in New York State, many people were studying and talking about the best way to follow Jesus Christ. There were many different Christian churches. Joseph wanted to know which church was Heavenly Father's true church. He visited all of them and studied the Bible, but he still didn't know which church he should join. One day, he read James 1:5: "If any of you lack wisdom, let him ask of God." Joseph knew in his heart that Heavenly Father would give him the guidance he needed.

When Joseph prayed to know which church was true, Heavenly Father and Jesus Christ appeared to him. They told him not to join any of the churches. They promised to send him more guidance (see Joseph Smith History 1:1–20).

Through the power of God, Joseph Smith organized the true Church of Jesus Christ.

Thought question: Have you ever prayed for knowledge, like Joseph Smith? How has Heavenly Father answered your prayers?

Visual Aid:

GAB 90/ GAK 403: The First Vision

2. Joseph Smith Translated the Book of Mormon by the Power of God

Have you ever seen words written in a language like Korean or Japanese? People who speak those languages use a different set of symbols to write than we do. If no one has taught you how to read that sort of writing, you couldn't even sound out the first word. And you wouldn't have any idea what the words meant.

When Joseph Smith received the golden plates, they were written in symbols that he couldn't read. In fact, no one in the world could read those symbols! There was only one way the Prophet Joseph could bring us the Book of Mormon: through the power of God. When Joseph was humble and righteous, Heavenly Father helped him translate the unfamiliar language on the plates.

Thought question: Share your feelings about the Book of Mormon and the Prophet Joseph Smith.

Scripture

D&C 20:8 — And gave him power from on high, by the means which were before prepared, to translate the Book of Mormon.

Visual Aid:

GAB 92: Joseph Smith Translating the Book of Mormon/ GAK 416: Translating the Book of Mormon

3. Jesus Christ's True Church Needed to be Restored

Scripture

2 Nephi 3:24 — And there shall rise up one mighty among them, who shall do much good, both in word and in deed, being an instrument in the hands of God, with exceeding faith, to work mighty wonders, and do that thing which is great in the sight of God, unto the bringing to pass much restoration unto the house of Israel, and unto the seed of thy brethren.

Visual Aid:

GAB 90/ GAK 403: The First Vision

When Jesus Christ was on the earth, He taught His gospel. He also gave His apostles His priesthood. But after the Savior died, was resurrected, and returned to heaven, people on earth started changing His true church. People outside the Church hurt and killed Jesus' followers. People inside the Church changed the teachings. After less than one hundred years had passed, the Church had changed so much that Heavenly Father took away the priesthood.

People still loved Jesus and wanted to follow Him. They started many Christian churches with all sorts of different teachings. But none of the churches had a prophet who could communicate with God. None of them had the priesthood ordinances that they needed to return to Heavenly Father. No one could belong to the true Church until the Savior brought it back again through the Prophet Joseph Smith.

Thought question: Why is it important to belong to Jesus Christ's true Church?

4. Line upon Line

When Joseph Smith restored the true Church of Jesus Christ, God didn't give him the entire gospel all at once. Instead, He gave it "live upon line" (D&C 98:12), or a little at a time. For example, one day while Joseph Smith and Oliver Cowdery were translating the Book of Mormon, they read about baptism. They wanted to be baptized, but they didn't know how to do it or if they even had the proper authority. So they went to the woods to pray. John the Baptist appeared. He ordained them to the Aaronic priesthood and told them to baptize each other. He also told them that they would have to wait until they received the Melchizedek priesthood to receive the gift of the Holy Ghost (see Joseph Smith—History 1:68–69).

Little by little, question by question, God restored His gospel through Joseph Smith.

Thought question: Have you ever come to understand an idea or doctrine "line upon line," like Joseph Smith?

Scripture

D&C 98:12 — For he will give unto the faithful line upon line, precept upon precept; and I will try you and prove you herewith.

Visual Aid:

GAB 93/ GAK 407: John the Baptist Conferring the Aaronic Priesthood

Chapter 5

The First Principles and Ordinances of the Gospel

1. Faith

Scripture

Article of Faith 1:4 — We believe that the first principles and ordinances of the Gospel are, first, Faith in the Lord Jesus Christ; second, Repentance; third, Baptism by immersion for the remission of sins; and fourth, Laying on of hands for the gift of the Holy Ghost.

A woman in New York City had met with the missionaries many years before, but she hadn't been baptized. Years later, she felt the Spirit tell her that she should talk to the missionaries again. She saw them in the crowded street, but she couldn't reach them in time. So she went home and prayed for them to come and teach her.

At the same time, two faithful missionaries looked at the old teaching records for their area. They found the woman's name. They went to visit her the same day she prayed to see them.

Because of faith—the woman's and the missionaries'—she learned the gospel and received baptism.[2]

Thought question: How did faith change lives in this story?

Visual Aid:

GAB 111/ GAK 605: Young Boy Praying

2. Repentance

Saul was a Jewish leader in Jesus' time. He did not believe that Jesus Christ was the Savior. He believed that the Christians were wicked. He went from town to town, preaching against the Christians and trying to destroy Jesus' Church. He even stood and watched while other wicked people killed one of Jesus' disciples.

Saul was walking to the city of Damascus to arrest Church members when, suddenly, he saw a bright light. He fell to the ground, and Jesus Christ's voice told him to stop what he was doing. When the light went away, Saul was blind. A Christian in Damascus healed him by the power of God (see Acts 9).

Saul changed his name to Paul and became a great missionary. Like Paul, we can all repent and serve Heavenly Father.

Thought question: How has repentance blessed your life?

Scripture
Mosiah 27:24 — I have repented of my sins, and have been redeemed of the Lord.

Visual Aid:
GAB 111/ GAK 605: Young Boy Praying

3. Baptism

Scripture

Moses 6:59 — Inasmuch as ye were born into the world by water, and blood, and the spirit, which I have made, and so became of dust a living soul, even so ye must be born again into the kingdom of heaven, of water, and of the Spirit, and be cleansed by blood, even the blood of mine Only Begotten.

Visual Aid:

GAB 104: Girl being baptized/ GAK 601: Baptism

After God cast Adam and Eve out of the Garden of Eden, He commanded them to be baptized. Adam didn't know why, so he prayed and asked. The Lord revealed to Adam that Jesus Christ would come to save all people from their sins. He taught Adam about the plan of salvation. He taught Adam that he must be "born again" (Moses 6:59) through Jesus' sacrifice. Adam rejoiced when he learned that, through Jesus Christ, he and all his children could be forgiven of their sins and return to Heavenly Father. They could receive the Holy Ghost to guide them home. Then the Spirit carried Adam under the water and baptized him (see Moses 6:53–68).

We are all "born again" like Adam when we are baptized. We covenant to accept Jesus' sacrifice so we can return to Heavenly Father.

Thought question: Why is it so important to covenant through baptism that we accept Jesus Christ's sacrifice for us?

4. The Gift of the Holy Ghost

After Jesus died, His disciples were gathered together. They had heard about the empty tomb, and Mary Magdalene had testified of His Resurrection. But they had not seen Him. As they spoke of Him, He appeared to them. He showed them His wounded hands and feet and side. He told them, "Peace be unto you."

Then He promised them a wonderful gift: the gift of the Holy Ghost. He would not be with them any more, but through the Holy Ghost, they could feel His love and receive His help. The Holy Ghost would give them peace. He commanded them to share this gift with all His children (see John 20:1–23).

We can all receive Jesus' gift through the ordinance of confirmation.

Thought question: What blessings come through the gift of the Holy Ghost?

Scripture

Acts 2:38 — Then Peter said unto them, Repent, and be baptized every one of you in the name of Jesus Christ for the remission of sins, and ye shall receive the gift of the Holy Ghost.

Visual Aid:

GAB 105/ GAK 602: The Gift of the Holy Ghost

Chapter 6

The Holy Ghost

1. The Holy Ghost

In the first Article of Faith, we say, "We believe in God the Eternal Father, and in His Son, Jesus Christ, and in the Holy Ghost." These are the three members of the Godhead. Each one has different responsibilities, but the three of them work together perfectly to bless Heavenly Father's children and to help us return home to live with God.

The Holy Ghost is the third member of the Godhead. Heavenly Father and Jesus Christ both have bodies with flesh and bones. But the Holy Ghost has no body. This allows Him to "dwell in us" (D&C 130:22). A person who is confirmed and receives the gift of the Holy Ghost can have His help to know what to do. He will teach us, comfort us, guide us, give us peace, answer our prayers, and help us feel and show love for Heavenly Father's children.

Thought question:
How has the Holy Ghost helped and blessed you or someone you know?

Scripture

D&C 130:22 — The Father has a body of flesh and bones as tangible as man's; the Son also; but the Holy Ghost has not a body of flesh and bones, but is a personage of Spirit. Were it not so, the Holy Ghost could not dwell in us.

Visual Aid:

GAB 105/ GAK 602: The Gift of the Holy Ghost

2. The Still, Small Voice

Elder Allan F. Packer played football as a young man. His coach made the team work very hard, and they had to do exactly what the coach told them to do. They learned to obey the coach instantly whenever he shouted directions across the field.

When Elder Packer played in a game against their team's biggest rival, there was a lot more noise than in practice: the crowd was yelling, the band was playing, the cheerleaders were shouting. But he had learned to listen to the coach. When the coach yelled, "Packer, tackle him!" young Elder Packer heard him clearly and made the wining tackle.[3]

Elder Packer said we need to learn what the voice of the Holy Ghost sounds like in our hearts. Then, even when other temptations and ideas are trying to get our attention, we can obey, believe, and be safe.

Thought question: Describe an experience with the Holy Ghost's power.

Scripture
Helaman 5:30 — And it came to pass when they heard this voice, and beheld that it was not a voice of thunder, neither was it a voice of a great tumultuous noise, but behold, it was a still voice of perfect mildness, as if it had been a whisper, and it did pierce even to the very soul.

Visual Aid:
None

3. The Arms of Safety

Scripture

3 Nephi 4:30 — May the God of Abraham, and the God of Isaac, and the God of Jacob, protect this people in righteousness, so long as they shall call on the name of their God for protection.

A nineteen-year-old man, named Ian, was visiting the Grand Canyon with his family when they heard shouts. A two-year-old girl had fallen over the railing to a narrow ledge. When she tried to climb back up to her family, she fell even farther. Ian, who had emergency training, knew what he had to do. He found a way down the cliff to the little girl. Then he held her tight until emergency crews lowered ropes to rescue them.[4]

Just as Ian held the little girl, Heavenly Father promises to "encircle [us] in the arms of safety" (Alma 34:16) if we will follow the Spirit's whispers in our hearts.

Thought question: How has the Spirit guided or protected you?

Visual Aid:
None

34

4. Ye May Know the Truth of All Things

Elder Neil L. Andersen was talking to a discouraged missionary who wanted to go home. The missionary said, "I don't even know if God loves me." But the Spirit told Elder Andersen that the missionary knew, deep in his heart, that God loved him.

Elder Andersen told the missionary, "I must correct you on one thing: you do know God loves you. You know He does." The Spirit spoke to the missionary's heart. He knew then that God loved him. Because he knew that, he was able to stay and work hard on his mission, even though it was still hard for him.[5]

The Book of Mormon prophet Moroni promises that we can "know the truth of all things" (Moroni 10:5). When we pray and study in faith, we can receive knowledge through the Holy Ghost

Thought question: How has the Spirit spoken in your heart and mind?

Scripture

Moroni 10:5 — And by the power of the Holy Ghost ye may know the truth of all things.

Visual Aid:

GAB 86/ GAK 320: Moroni hides the plates in the Hill Cumorah

Chapter 7

Following Jesus Christ's Example

1. Jesus Obeyed His Father in Heaven

Scripture

Matthew 26:39 — And he went a little further, and fell on his face, and prayed, saying, O my Father, if it be possible, let this cup pass from me: nevertheless not as I will, but as thou wilt.

Before the world was created, we all lived with Heavenly Father as His spirit children. He taught us the plan of salvation, and we were so happy we shouted for joy. He said that we would need a savior: someone who would die for us to save us from our sins. Without a savior, we would not be able to return home to Heavenly Father. Satan wanted glory by being our savior, but he had a plan that would destroy our agency. Jesus said, "Father, thy will be done," and Heavenly Father chose Him as our Savior (see Moses 4:1–4).

Jesus obeyed Heavenly Father's plan. Even when He was suffering unimaginable pain for our sins, He still said, "Not my will, but thine be done" (Luke 22:42). We can follow Jesus by obeying Heavenly Father, even when it seems very difficult.

Visual Aid:

GAB 56/ GAK 227: Jesus Praying in Gethsemane

Thought question: What can you do to obey Heavenly Father's will?

2. Jesus Christ Served Others

When Jesus Christ was on the earth, He had a body like ours: He got hungry and thirsty, He felt heat and cold and pain, and He got tired like we do. When a wicked king killed John the Baptist, Jesus was very sad. He took His apostles to a private place. But the people wouldn't leave Him alone. Some loved Him and wanted to be with Him. Some just wanted to see Him perform miracles.

Most people would complain or get angry if someone wouldn't let them be alone when they were sad and weary. But not Jesus. He went out and taught the people. When they got hungry, he miraculously gave them bread and fish to eat (see Mark 6:30–44).

Before He suffered and died for all of us, Jesus sacrificed His own rest and comfort to bless Heavenly Father's children.

Thought question: How can you follow Jesus' example of serving others?

Scripture

Mark 6:34 — And Jesus, when he came out, saw much people, and was moved with compassion toward them, because they were as sheep not having a shepherd: and he began to teach them many things.

Visual Aid:

GAB 39/ GAK 212: The Sermon on the Mount

3. I Can Follow Jesus' Example by Not Judging

Scripture

John 8:7 — So when they continued asking him, he lifted up himself, and said unto them, He that is without sin among you, let him first cast a stone at her.

When Jesus lived in Jerusalem, the leaders who didn't like Him often tried to catch Him making a mistake. One day, they found a woman who had committed a serious sin. They dragged her over to Him and asked Him what to do with her. No matter what He said, they planned to use His words against Him.

Jesus was not upset or frightened. He said, "He that is without sin among you, let him first cast a stone at her" (John 8:7). Then He calmly wrote on the ground. Everyone suddenly felt very uncomfortable. They all knew they weren't perfect, either. One by one, they all went away, until only Jesus and the woman were left. He forgave her of her sins and told her to sin no more (see John 8:1–11).

We can follow Jesus' example by refusing to judge others.

Thought question: How do you feel when someone treats you with kindness and understanding?

Visual Aid:

GAB 1: Jesus Christ/ GAK 240 Jesus the Christ

4. I Can Follow Jesus Christ's Example by Thinking About Others

When Jesus was crucified, women who followed Him gathered at the foot of the cross, weeping. Jesus's mother, Mary, was there, with His apostle, John. Jesus said to His mother, "Woman, behold thy son!" Then He said to John, "Behold thy mother!" (John 19:25–27). After Jesus' death, John took Mary to his house and cared for her. Even though He was in terrible pain Himself, the Savior wanted to make sure that someone took care of His mother.

Everyone has their own pain and troubles, but no one suffers worse than how the Savior suffered for us. We can follow His example by looking for others to help, even when we have problems ourselves.

Thought question: How has someone helped you? How have you helped someone else?

Scripture

Acts 10:38 — How God anointed Jesus of Nazareth with the Holy Ghost and with power: who went about doing good, and healing all that were oppressed of the devil; for God was with him.

Visual Aid:

GAB 57/ GAK 230: The Crucifixion

Chapter 8

Jesus Christ Is a God of Miracles

1. Jesus Calms the Sea

Scripture

Mark 4:39 — And he arose, and rebuked the wind, and said unto the sea, Peace, be still. And the wind ceased, and there was a great calm.

One evening, Jesus and His disciples set out across the Sea of Galilee in a boat. Jesus went to sleep while His disciples sailed the ship. He was still sleeping when a great storm blew up. In the wind and the waves and the darkness, the disciples were afraid. They woke Jesus up in a panic. He stood and told the sea, "Peace, be still." The wind calmed down, and suddenly the storm ended. The disciples, who didn't yet understand that Jesus was the Son of God, were amazed at this miracle (see Mark 4:35–41).

Sometimes we get "stormy" inside: angry, or frightened, or worried, or discouraged. Just as He did with the Sea of Galilee, Jesus can calm an upset heart or mind if we let Him bring us the peace He promises.

Thought question: How have you felt peace through the gospel of Jesus Christ?

Visual Aid:

GAB 40: Jesus Calms the Sea/
GAK 214: Stilling the Storm

2. Jesus Heals a Man at the Pool of Bethesda

Jesus visited Jerusalem and saw many sick and hurt people near a pool called Bethesda. It was said that sometimes an angel came and rippled the water. Whoever reached the water first after that would be healed. One man there had been lying near the pool for thirty-eight years. Jesus asked him, "Wilt thou be made whole?" (John 5:6). The man answered that he wanted to be healed, but he had no one to help him, so someone else always reached the water before he did. Jesus told the man to stand up, pick up his sleeping mat, and walk. The man was healed at once (see John 5:1–9).

President Thomas S. Monson said, "At Bethesda He took compassion on the crippled man who had no hope to get to the pool of promise. He extended His hand; He lifted him up. He healed him."[6]

Thought question: How has the power of the priesthood healed you or someone you know?

Scripture

John 5:8–9 — Jesus saith unto him, rise, take up thy bed, and walk. And immediately the man was made whole, and took up his bed, and walked.

Visual Aid:

GAB 42: Christ Healing the Sick at Bethesda

3. Jesus Raises Lazarus from the Dead

Scripture

John 11:25 — Jesus said unto her, I am the resurrection, and the life: he that believeth in me, though he were dead, yet shall he live.

Jesus' three friends Mary, Martha, and Lazarus lived in the city of Bethany. They were two sisters and a brother. Lazarus got very sick, and Mary and Martha sent Jesus a message, asking Him to come and heal their brother. Instead of going right away, Jesus stayed two more days where He was. When He finally arrived at Mary's and Martha's house, Lazarus had been dead for four days.

Jesus asked Martha if she believed in Him. Martha testified that Jesus was the Savior and the Son of God. But she and Mary were still surprised when Jesus told them to open the tomb. He called into the tomb with a loud voice, "Lazarus, come forth!" And Lazarus walked out, still wrapped in the burial cloths. Jesus showed the people that, as the Son of God, He had power over death (see John 11:1–47).

Visual Aid:

GAB 49: Jesus Raising Lazarus from the Dead

Thought question: Share how you feel knowing that you will be resurrected through the power of Jesus Christ's Atonement.

4. Miracles Come by Faith

The four sons of Mosiah in the Book of Mormon wanted to preach the gospel to the wicked Lamanites. Their father, King Mosiah, was growing old. He probably knew that he might not see his sons again. He also knew that the Lamanites were very dangerous, so he prayed about his decision. God told him to let his sons go and promised to protect them. He also promised Mosiah that his sons would teach and convert many of the Lamanites (see Mosiah 28:1–9).

King Mosiah died before his sons returned home, but the Lord's promises to them were fulfilled. The Lamanites tried to kill them many times, but they were always kept safe. Thousands of the Lamanites repented of their sins and accepted the gospel of Jesus Christ. Through faith—King Mosiah's faith, his sons' faith, and the Lamanites' faith—God performed great miracles (see Alma 17–26).

Thought question: How has faith led to miracles in your life or in the life of someone you know?

Scripture

Alma 19:23 — Now we see that Ammon could not be slain, for the Lord had said unto Mosiah, his father: I will spare him, and it shall be unto him according to thy faith—therefore, Mosiah trusted him unto the Lord.

Visual Aid:

GAB 78/ GAK 310: Ammon defends the flocks of King Lamoni

Chapter 9

If Ye Love Me, Keep My Commandments

1. Preparing for a Mission Shows My Love for Jesus Christ

Scripture

1 Samuel 7:3 — Prepare your hearts unto the Lord, and serve him only.

Elder Ulisses Soares grew up in South America. One day, the bishop called him into his office and told him to start preparing for a mission right away. Ulisses was surprised—he was only eleven years old! But the bishop promised that Ulisses would serve a mission if he started preparing by keeping the commandments, honoring the priesthood, staying worthy, and being honest. Ulisses promised, and he tried hard to keep his promise.

When he was in high school, he worked hard to pay for his mission. Each month, he paid his tithing, then bought one piece of clothing he would need for his mission: a tie, a shirt, a belt.

When the time came, Ulisses was ready for his mission, because he had obeyed counsel his bishop gave when he was eleven.[7]

Thought question: How has keeping the commandments increased your love for Jesus Christ?

Visual Aid:

GAB 113: Payment of Tithing

2. Showing Gratitude Shows My Love for Jesus Christ

When Elder Joseph B. Wirthlin was a young man, he played on his school's football team. One day, he came home discouraged and unhappy because his team had lost the game. His mother sat down with him and listened to his troubles. Then she said, "Joseph, come what may, and love it."

Elder Wirthlin said that, even when we have problems, we can find joy if we learn to laugh, seek for the eternal lessons we're learning, trust that the Lord will make up all the bad things that happen to us, and trust in our Heavenly Father.[8] God has commanded us to "[give] thanks always" (Ephesians 5:20)—not just for good things and happy times. Showing gratitude shows our love for Jesus Christ

Thought question: Think about a hard or discouraging time in your life. List some blessings that came from that time.

Scripture

Ephesians 5:20 — Giving thanks always for all things unto God and the Father in the name of our Lord Jesus Christ.

Visual Aid:

None

3. My Love for Jesus Christ Grows When I Pray

Scripture

D&C 19:38 — Pray always, and I will pour out my Spirit upon you, and great shall be your blessing—yea, even more than if you should obtain treasures of earth.

President Dieter F. Uchtdorf was a small living child in Europe when World War II started. His father was drafted into the army, and the war was getting closer to their home every day. His mother decided to take her four children and go live with relatives in Germany. The trip on the train was cold and dangerous. When the train stopped, Elder Uchtdorf's mother got off to find some food for her family. But when she got back to the station, the train—with all her children on it—was gone!

She prayed frantically. Then, clinging to hope, she searched up and down the station, checking every track and every train. Elder Uchtdorf said, "She put her faith and hope into action," until at last she found her family.[9]

Thought question: How have prayer and hope helped you or someone you know?

Visual Aid:

GAB 112/ GAK 606: Family Prayer

4. The Scriptures Teach of Jesus Christ

One day when Jesus was teaching the people, some of the parents brought their children to receive blessing from Jesus. The disciples told them to take the children away, since Jesus had already said that little children are saved and need no repentance. But Jesus called the children back. He took the children into His arms and blessed each one of them (see Mark 10:13–16).

We can learn about Jesus from the scriptures. As we read, the Spirit will testify that the scriptures are true and help us feel closer to the Savior.

Thought question: Think about how you would feel if you were one of the children that Jesus took in His arms. Share your feelings.

Scripture

John 5:39 — Search the scriptures; for in them ye think ye have eternal life: and they are they which testify of me.

Visual Aid:

GAB 116: Christ with Children/ GAK 608: Christ and Children from around the World

Chapter 10

Come Unto Christ

1. A Reverence Tent for General Conference

Scripture

Mosiah 2:9 — Hearken unto me, and open your ears that ye may hear, and your hearts that ye may understand, and your minds that the mysteries of God may be unfolded to your view.

Braydon and Elise were reading about King Benjamin's speech in the Book of Mormon during family scripture time. Elise suddenly got a great idea. What if they set up a tent just like the people in King Benjamin's time? Those people brought their tents to the temple and listened to the prophets with their families. General conference was the next day. Braydon and Elise could do the same thing!

While the kids built a tent-fort out of tables, blankets, and sofa cushions, Mom gathered crayons, paper, and glue sticks. The kids could draw pictures, take notes, and cut out pictures of the apostles to glue to their notes. They called it the "conference reverence tent," so everyone would remember to listen carefully to the words of the prophets.[10]

Thought question: What could you do to help your family listen more carefully to general conference?

Visual Aid:

GAB 74/ GAK 307: King Benjamin Addresses His People

2. Inviting Others to Come Unto Christ

For many years, the Lamanites had hated and tried to kill the Nephites. But the sons of King Mosiah were determined to share the gospel with the Lamanites. Ammon went to the land of the Lamanite King Lamoni and offered to be his servant. Lamoni sent Ammon out to tend the sheep. When wicked men came to scatter the sheep, the other servants ran away, but Ammon stayed and defended the flocks with power from God.

King Lamoni couldn't believe how humble and faithful Ammon was. He even thought that Ammon might be God! He asked Ammon to tell him how he had become so powerful. Ammon taught him about Heavenly Father, the Atonement of Jesus Christ, and the plan of salvation. The king and many of the people in his kingdom believed, repented, and were baptized because Ammon was brave and set a good example (see Alma 17–18).

Thought question: Who could you invite to come unto Christ? How could you do it?

Scripture

2 Nephi 26:33 — He doeth nothing save it be plain unto the children of men; and he inviteth them all to come unto him and partake of his goodness; and he denieth none that come unto him, black and white, bond and free, male and female.

Visual Aid:

GAB 78/ GAK 310: Ammon Defends the Flocks of King Lamoni

3. Coming Unto Christ by Repenting

Scripture

3 Nephi 9:22 — Therefore, whoso repenteth and cometh unto me as a little child, him will I receive, for of such is the kingdom of God. Behold, for such I have laid down my life, and have taken it up again; therefore repent, and come unto me ye ends of the earth, and be saved.

Visual Aid:

None

Billy's grandma had a mirror that had belonged to a pioneer ancestor. When she was crossing the plains, she would look in the mirror after a long, difficult day and remember that she was seeing a daughter of God.

Billy wanted to look in the mirror on the shelf, and his brother tried to help him. But together they broke the shelf and spilled Grandma's plant. They planned to blame the accident on the cat, but at dinner, they both felt terrible. Finally, they told Grandma. Neither boy felt much like a child of God. But Grandma reminded them that they were always children of God. And Dad also reminded them that they didn't blame the cat, even though they were tempted to. Billy looked in the mirror. He saw a child of God with a good feeling inside, who was grateful for the blessing of repentance.[11]

Thought question: How has repentance blessed you or someone you know?

4. Touching the temple

Eliza was frustrated. Her two brothers were old enough to do baptisms for the dead in the temple, but she was only ten. Her mother promised to stay outside with her, and together they could touch the temple. This sounded like a silly idea to Eliza. Touching the temple didn't sound nearly as good as getting to go inside.

After the boys went downstairs to the baptistry, Eliza and her mother walked around the temple grounds. They enjoyed the peaceful feeling there, watched the fountain, and waved to the Angel Moroni. Then they walked up and pressed their hands against the temple wall. A strong, sacred feeling flooded into each of them. Eliza and her mother looked at each other in surprise. Eliza realized that, even if she couldn't go inside the temple, she could still feel its sweet power in her life.[12]

Thought question: How can the temple touch your life before you're old enough to go inside?

Scripture

D&C 97:15–16 — And inasmuch as my people build a house unto me in the name of the Lord, and do not suffer any unclean thing to come into it, that it be not defiled, my glory shall rest upon it; Yea, and my presence shall be there, for I will come into it, and all the pure in heart that shall come into it shall see God.

Visual Aid:

GAB 119/ GAK 502: Salt Lake Temple, or a picture of your local temple.

Chapter 11

When You Are in the Service of Your Fellow Beings, You Are Only in the Service of Your God

1. Jesus Christ's Example of Service: Washing the Apostles' Feet

Scripture

John 13:14 — If I then, your Lord and Master, have washed your feet; ye also ought to wash one another's feet.

The night before Jesus was crucified, He and His apostles gathered to eat the Passover dinner. Jesus introduced the sacrament to them. Then He got a bowl of water and tied a towel around His waist. He started washing the apostles' feet. At first, the apostle Peter did not want Jesus to wash his feet, since Jesus was the Lord and washing feet was a servant's job. But Jesus explained that Peter had to let the Lord serve him.

Later Jesus taught them that He washed their feet to set the example: if the Lord Himself serves us, then we ought to serve each other (see John 13:1–15).

Thought question: How can you serve someone else? How does service follow Jesus Christ's example?

Visual Aid:

GAB 55/ GAK 226: Jesus washing the Apostles' Feet

2. Jesus Christ's Example of Service: "Feed My Sheep"

After Jesus Christ was resurrected, He appeared to His disciples while they were fishing in their boats. He cooked them dinner on the beach, and then He asked Peter, "Lovest thou me?" Peter said yes, he loved the Lord. Then Jesus said, "Feed my lambs." This happened two more times, and Peter was beginning to feel frustrated. Why did the Lord keep asking? He kept asking, because the answer was very important.

When Jesus talks about lambs or sheep, He is talking about Heavenly Father's children. If we love the Savior, we must show it by sharing with others, telling them about the Church, serving them, and treating them kindly. Then we will be keeping the commandment that Jesus gave to Peter and to all of us.

Thought question: How can you serve Heavenly Father's children?

Scripture

John 21:15 — So when they had dined, Jesus saith to Simon Peter, Simon, son of Jonas, lovest thou me more than these? He saith unto him, Yeah, Lord; thou knowest that I love thee. He saith unto him, Feed my lambs.

Visual Aid:

GAB 64: The Lost Lamb/ GAK 240: Jesus the Christ

3. Lift Where You Stand in Your Family

Scripture

Mosiah 2:17 — And I tell you these things that ye may learn wisdom; that ye may learn that when ye are in the service of your fellow beings ye are only in the service of your God.

Visual Aid:

GAB 112/ GAK 606: Family Prayer

President Dieter F. Uchtdorf told a story about a group of men who wanted to move a grand piano from one room of the church to another. They tried pushing and pulling and many other ideas, but they simply couldn't move that piano. Then one man suggested, "Brethren, stand close together and lift where you stand." It almost seemed too easy, but when they tried it, it worked! They carried the piano all the way to the next room.[13]

In our families, everyone has responsibilities. If we try to tell each other what to do, or criticize the jobs that others are doing, our families have trouble and we don't get very far. But if we do our best at our own responsibilities and try hard to help each other, we can make great progress and have fun, too!

Thought question: How can you serve in your family this week?

4. Serving Others, Serving God

Phil lost his job as a mechanic, and he was having trouble finding a new job. His elders quorum and the ward leaders got together and figured out that Phil could start his own auto mechanic business, if they gave him some help. One ward member donated an old barn. Others found tools and equipment and fixed up the barn. Soon, Phil was able to start working as a mechanic again. His business was so successful that he soon had to move to a better building.[14]

As children of God and as members of a ward, we can help others who are in trouble. We can also let others help us when we need it. When we serve God's children, we also serve our Heavenly Father.

Thought question: How have people in your ward or neighborhood served you? How can you serve them?

Scripture
Luke 22:32 — But I have prayed for thee, that thy faith fail not: and when thou art converted, strengthen thy brethren.

Visual Aid:
GAB 115: Service/ GAK 615: Serving One Another

Chapter 12

He Lives!

1. Samuel the Lamanite Prophesies about Jesus Christ

Scripture

Helaman 14:3 — There shall be great lights in heaven, insomuch that in the night before he cometh there shall be no darkness, insomuch that it shall appear unto man as if it was day.

A few years before Jesus was born, God sent Samuel, a Lamanite, to testify to the Nephites about Jesus Christ. Samuel told them that, when Jesus was born, there would be a day and a night and a day with no darkness. A new star would appear in the sky, and the people would see many wonderful things in the heavens.

The wicked Nephites chased Samuel out of the city and tried to kill him. They even decided to kill the people who believed in Jesus Christ, if the signs did not come.

The righteous people prayed and hoped for the sign of Jesus' birth, and it came, just as Samuel had prophesied. All the prophets since Adam had looked forward to Jesus' birth, and now it had finally come (see Helaman 13–15).

Thought question:
How would you feel if you lived two thousand years ago and you heard that the Savior had just been born?

Visual Aid:

GAB 81/ GAK 314: Samuel the Lamanite on the Wall

2. Jesus Christ Died to Save the World

The Old Testament prophet Ezekiel saw a vision of a huge valley covered in dried-out old bones. In the vision, the Lord came to Ezekiel and asked, "Can these bones live?" Then the Lord told the prophet to tell the bones to listen to the word of the Lord. When Ezekiel told the bones to listen, they started to shake. Then they came together and stood up. The Lord made them into living bodies and breathed life into them (See Ezekiel 37:1–14).

Ezekiel's prophecy taught him about the Resurrection. Every person on the earth will die, but because of Jesus' Atonement, everyone will be resurrected with a whole and perfect body. Those who have accepted and followed the Savior and repented of their sins will be able to live with Jesus, Heavenly Father, and their families forever.

Thought question: How do you feel when you imagine you and your family being resurrected?

Scripture

1 Corinthians 15:22 — For as in Adam all die, even so in Christ shall all be made alive.

Visual Aid:

GAB 3: The Earth/ GAK 600: The World

3. The Second Coming of Jesus Christ

Scripture

Isaiah 11:9 — They shall not hurt nor destroy in all my holy mountain: for the earth shall be full of the knowledge of the Lord, as the waters cover the sea.

Have you ever seen a lion or a tiger at the zoo? It was probably in a big, strong cage. It might eat you if it had the chance! Here on this earth, bigger, faster, stronger animals eat smaller, weaker ones. Stronger people often hurt weaker ones, too.

Someday, Jesus Christ will return to the earth. The scriptures tell us what the world will be like then. We will have peace: no wars, no violence, no fighting. Animals will not hurt each other. Even a wolf and a bear and a lamb could play together, and children would not have to be afraid of them (see Isaiah 11:6–9).

The time when Jesus returns will be joyful for the people who have prepared. We don't know when He will come, so we have to live well all the time, so we will be ready.

Thought question: What can you do today to get ready for Jesus' Second Coming?

Visual Aid:

GAB 66/ GAK 238: The Second Coming

4. A Lively Hope

A church leader visited Peru after a huge earthquake there. He met with the stake president and his wife as they were helping with the cleanup and rescue. The stake president's wife was carrying one of her children, and she was smiling. Their family had all survived, but their house and everything they owned had been destroyed. She told the leader, "I have prayed and I am at peace. We have all we need. We have each other, we have our children, we are sealed in the temple, we have this marvelous Church, and we have the Lord."[15]

Someday, if we are righteous and trust in the Savior, we can live with Him again. But we can be joyful and hopeful now, because He has given us the gospel and the gift of the Holy Ghost to lead and comfort us.

Thought question: How does the gospel bless you right now?

Scripture

1 Peter 1:3 — Blessed be the God and Father of our Lord Jesus Christ, which according to his abundant mercy hath begotten us again unto a lively hope by the resurrection of Jesus Christ from the dead.

Visual Aid:

GAB 1: Jesus Christ/ GAK 240: Jesus the Christ

References

1. Personal communication, used by permission

2. Thomas S. Monson, "Be Your Best Self," *Ensign*, May 2009, 67–70.

3. Allan F. Packer, "Finding Strength in Challenging Times!" *Ensign*, May 2009, 17–19.

4. Patricia Auxier, "Save Her!" *New Era*, Sep. 2007, 7–8.

5. Neil L. Andersen, "You Know Enough," *Ensign*, Nov. 2008, 13–14.

6. Thomas S. Monson, "The Way of the Master," *Ensign*, Jan. 2003, 5–7.

7. Ulisses Soares, "Preparing for a Mission," *Friend*, Oct. 2008, 9.

8. Joseph B. Wirthlin, "Come What May, and Love It," *Ensign*, Nov. 2008, 26–28.

9. Dieter F. Uchtdorf, "The Infinite Power of Hope," *Ensign*, Nov. 2008, 21–24.

10. Linda Olsen, "Conference Reverence Tent," *Friend*, Oct. 2008, 37–38.

11. Hazel Lamoreaux, "Seeing a Child of God," *Friend*, Nov. 2008, 5–6.

12. Personal communication with author, used by permission.

13. Dieter F. Uchtdorf, "Lift Where You Stand," *Ensign*, Nov. 2008, 53–56.

14. Richard C. Edgley, "This Is Your Phone Call," *Ensign*, May 2009, 53–55.

15. D. Todd Christofferson, "The Power of Covenants," *Ensign*, May 2009, 19–23.

About the Author

Lee Ann Setzer is raising a lively family of three children with her husband. When she's not writing, she likes to sew, read, and run model trains in the backyard with her family (the trains aren't big enough to ride on, though). Lee Ann is the author of three other *Tiny Talks* books, *I Am Ready for Baptism!*, and the Sariah McDuff chapter book series.